The Handbook for High Achievers

A Book For Winners

By

Bruce F. Wells

Printed in the United States of America
by Dlux Printing, Pensacola, Florida
Cover Design: Cissi Milford, 3SIXTY Designstudio
Interior Design: Kevin Rankin
Senior Editor: Deborah Wells, Ph.D.

This publication is designed to provide accurate information in regard to the subject matter covered. It is sold with the understanding that no legal, accounting or financial advice is offered. Every reasonable effort has been made to correctly quote and give credit to the individuals quoted.

Wells, Bruce
The Handbook For High Achievers
First Edition, 2015
ISBN: 978-0-578-15495-4

winningpublishing@gmail.com

Winning Publishing and Presentations
Gulf Breeze, Florida, USA

INTRODUCTION

Life has been good to me. Sometimes it has been challenging. Mostly it's been fun. I have been blessed with a good family and good health. Life experiences have given me an insight for advising friends and the younger generations. It's easy advice. Mainly, it's a conversation about honesty, integrity and a sense of humor. It must be acceptable guidance because I continue to receive calls from friends, peers and associates. Maybe it's just because I make them laugh. Regardless, I appreciate the confidence. I also enjoy the attention.

Life is not always easy. How you handle the challenge of its difficulties is what matters. It is a two-step process: define the problem; determine the solutions. Often it is that simple. However, sometimes it's not that easy. The best solutions are logical, not emotional. Try not to have a knee jerk reaction. Take your time. Finally, try to see the humor, even in difficult circumstances. I hope you enjoy my musings. Life is never perfect but it is an opportunity to enjoy. Just do the best you can.

Also By
Bruce F. Wells

Inside Technology Stocks
McGraw-Hill

All About Variable Annuities
From The Inside Out
McGraw-Hill

about the author...

Bruce F. Wells is a nationally recognized sales trainer, motivational speaker, humorist, writer and investment expert. He has served as a senior executive in the banking, insurance, mutual fund and securities industries. He is the author of the nationally distributed books, "All About Variable Annuities From The Inside Out" (A Money Book Club Selection) (McGraw Hill) and "Inside Technology Stocks" (McGraw-Hill). He is now a full-time lecturer and writer living in the Florida Panhandle.

DEDICATION

To Suzanne, the light of my life and the smartest and kindest person I know. To my children. You have made me happy both with your caring approach and your personal successes. To my personal and business friends for their kindness in calling. Finally, to my secret sage. While no longer with us, your advice and good humor still guide me.

A Book For Winners

Food for Thought

"A four-star restaurant will charge significantly more for a potato than a fast food establishment, but it's still a potato. The difference between selling a potato for ten dollars compared to a dollar is preparation, presentation, quality, atmosphere, service and customer expectations."

Bruce Wells

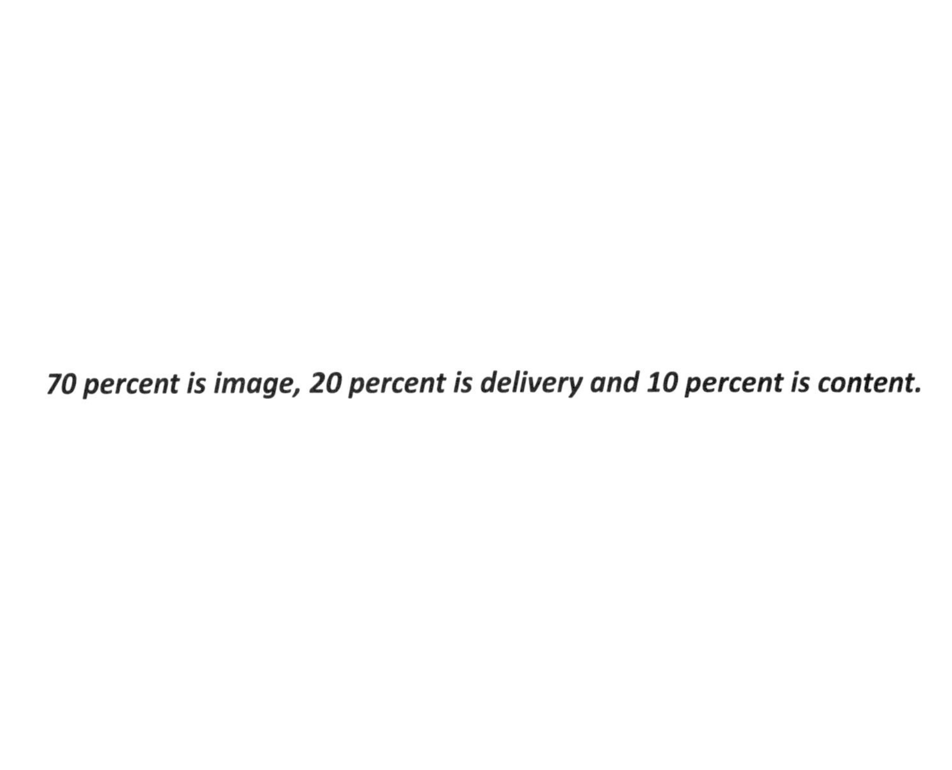

70 percent is image, 20 percent is delivery and 10 percent is content.

The ability to communicate effectively is an essential ingredient to your success, whether you are in sales, management, education, human resources, food service, auto repair, bartending, acting or any other occupation that interacts with the public. Your ability to effectively communicate, articulate, and project a warm, friendly, trusting demeanor will provide a direct link between your ability to persuade and your ability to be successful.

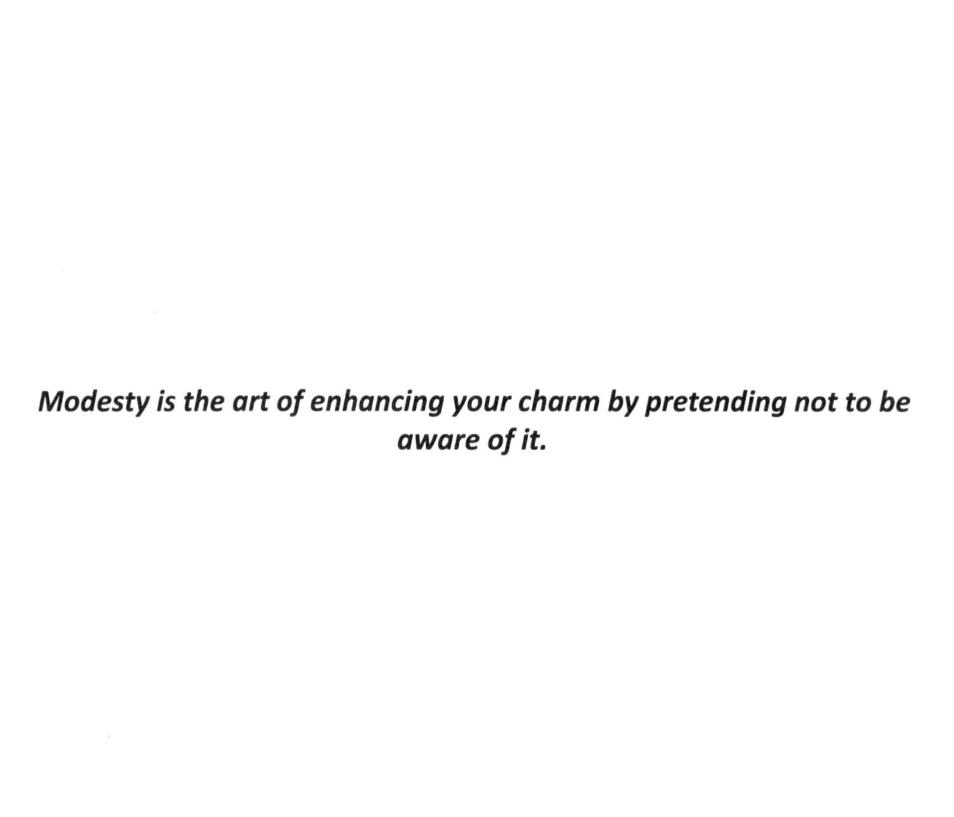

Modesty is the art of enhancing your charm by pretending not to be aware of it.

The traits of successful people are too numerous to mention but let's give it a try anyway. First, they are great communicators. Second, they build solid relationships and work well at all levels. Third, they self-manage. This includes practicing self-discipline, prioritizing responsibilities, maintaining a professional image, accepting responsibility and being completely honest.

Maintaining a dynamic appearance for every occasion shows you care.

BW

Career professionals should always be well groomed and well turned out whether at the grocery store or the country club. One should dress appropriately for all occasions. We live in a highly competitive world. You never know when you might run into the President or a former high school classmate. The four horsemen apply: clean, pressed, tucked and groomed. Even your "sloppy" look should appear neat to give you confidence and an edge.

We made too many wrong mistakes.
Yogi Berra

Accept responsibility. Nothing is more refreshing than an individual who steps forward and says “I am responsible, I messed up, I will fix it and I will try not to do it again.” Once folks recover from the shock of an individual displaying integrity, honesty and sincerity, that person will gain even more respect as a stand-up person. The problem also disappears much more quickly.

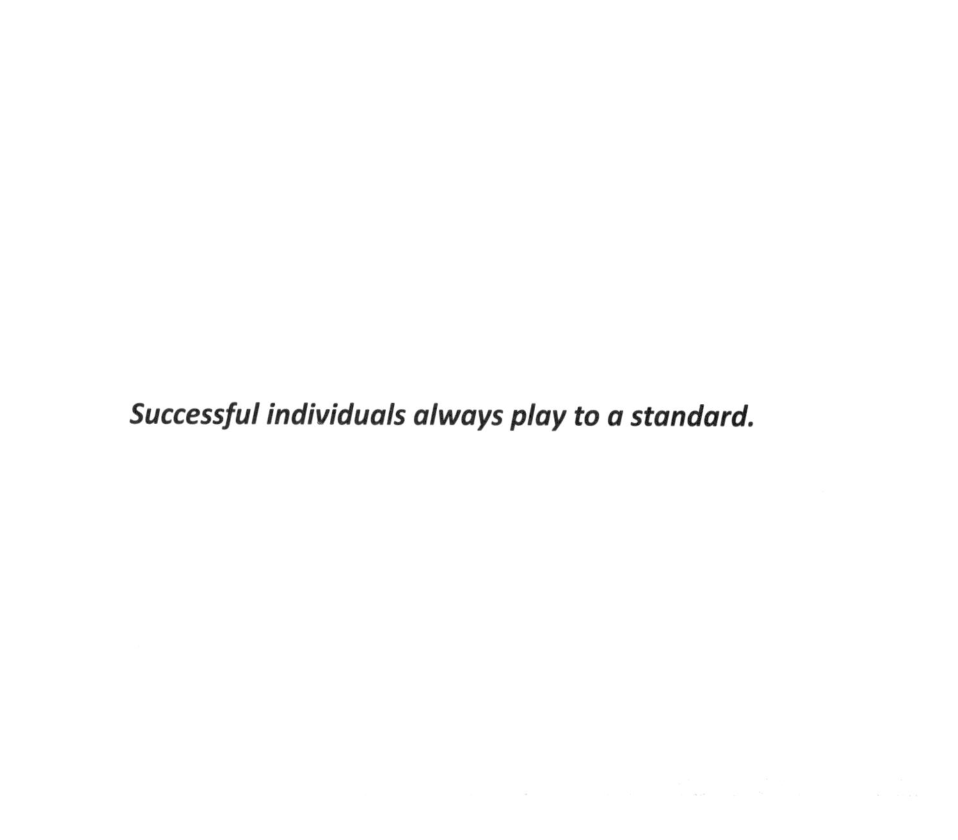

Successful individuals always play to a standard.

Each day practice the skill sets required for you to be successful. An ease of conversation that demonstrates your acumen and professionalism sets you apart from the competition. As Tony Bennett (among others) said, “If I don’t practice the first day, I will know. If I don’t practice the second day, the orchestra will know. If I don’t practice the third day, the audience will know.” He also said “develop your own style.” Words of wisdom from an American icon.

It has been demonstrated time and again that organizations and individuals that engage in systematic planning have better success records than those who do not.

Lester R. Bittel

Highly effective strategies define the primary objective, concentrate assets, determine the highest and best use of personnel, and identify a clear line of authority (who is responsible for what). Most importantly, they maintain operational simplicity (everyone knows what to do and does it). It's required in the military and highly effective in private industry.

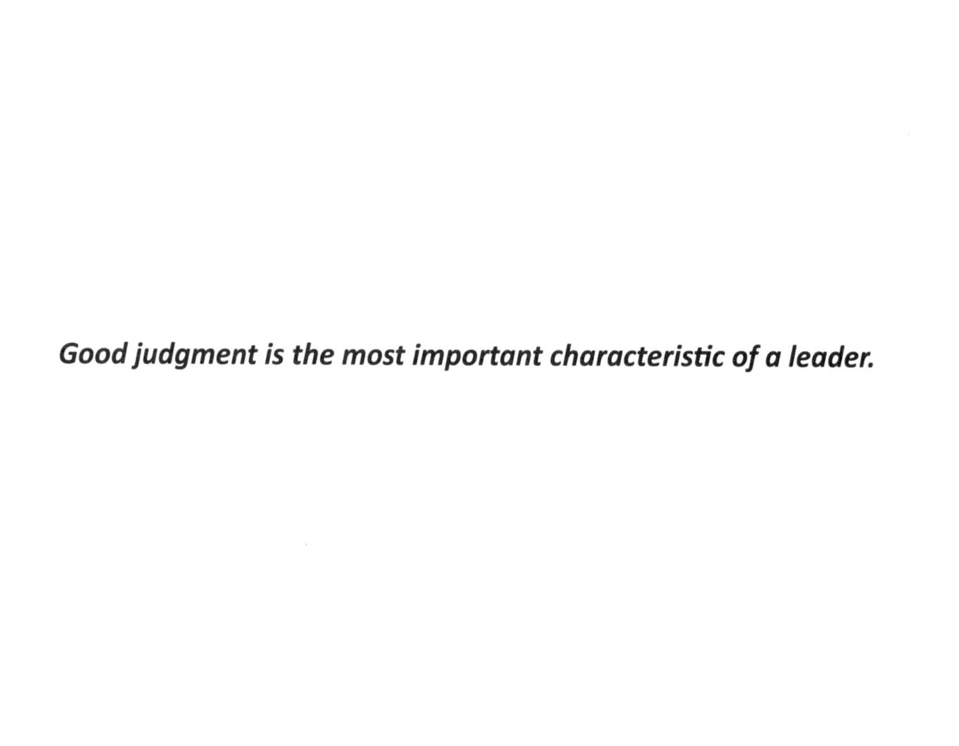

Good judgment is the most important characteristic of a leader.

There are two kinds of leaders: those who lead by inspiration and those who lead by intimidation. Inspirational leaders are most admired and most successful. Since it is all show business, it matters little if the leader is a method actor or is improvisational, reserved or ebullient. Any personality is acceptable as long as one strives to act in an intelligent manner and is objective, honest, competent, fair and cooperative.

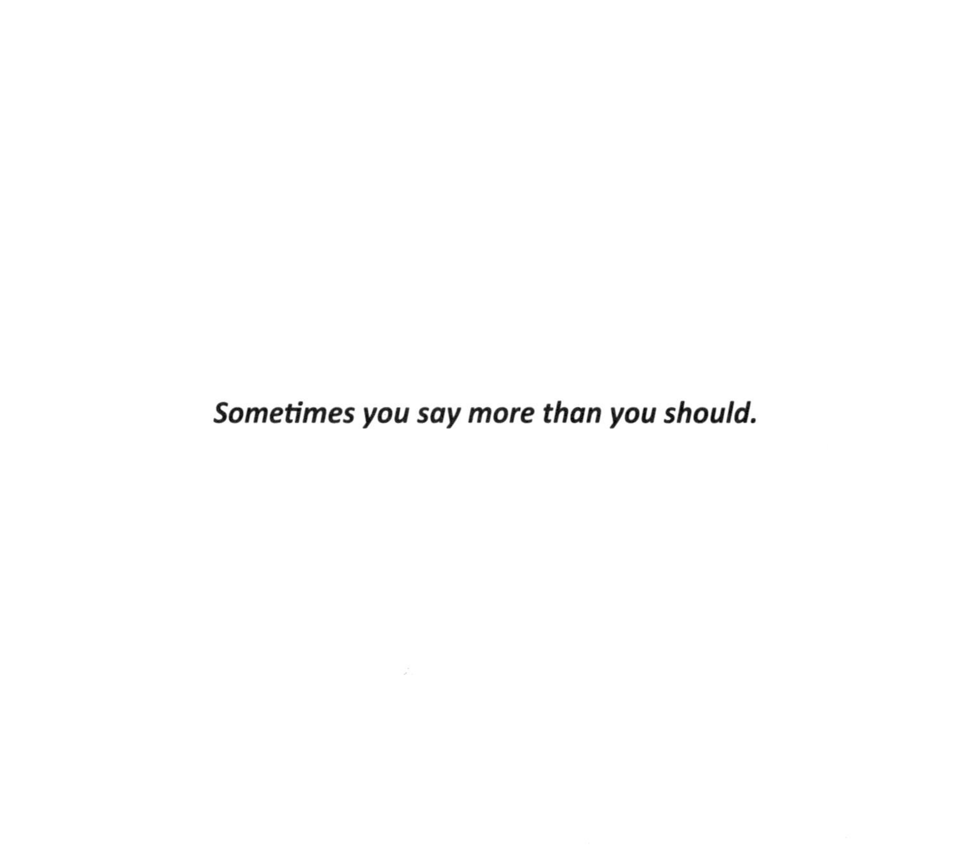

Sometimes you say more than you should.

The best advice you will receive is never lose your temper. Nothing positive ever comes from obnoxious behavior except people are positive you are exhibiting obnoxious behavior. This is not the action of a person seeking acceptance. This is the one strategy above all others that will earn you respect.

Show class, have pride and display character.
If you do, winning will take care of itself.
Coach Paul Bryant

Cultivate friends and associates who are winners. Success is contagious. It's OK to catch it. Your outlook will be happier. Your career and personal life will be more successful. Your relationships will grow and prosper. It's a fact; your contemporaries pay attention to the status of your friends and your associates.

To most golfers a handicap is a number. To some golfers, their handicap is their personality and lack of integrity.

BW

Play golf with an individual if you want to learn more about him. Duffers demonstrate their personalities, integrity and approach to life on the links. Beware of people who score better with a pencil than a putter. Admire the person who counts the strokes, plays their lie, bets modestly, if at all, and compliments the foursome by buying refreshments, when they win. That's a person of integrity who enjoys an honorable life experience.

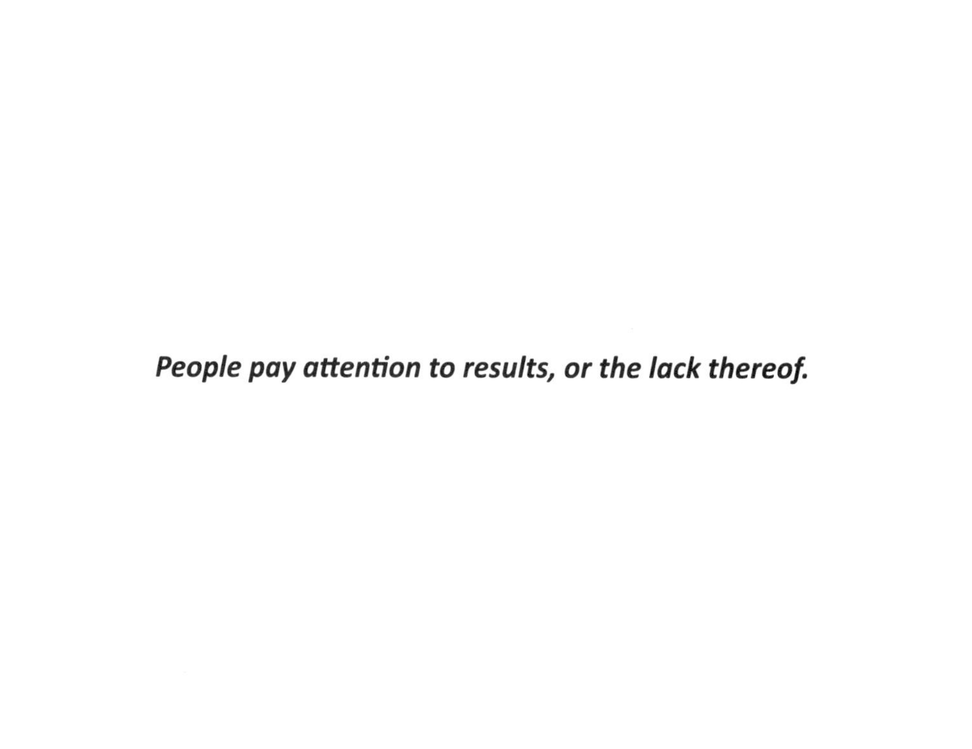

People pay attention to results, or the lack thereof.

Steve Jobs displayed a maniacal attention to details. Many credit this trait as the most important attribute that made him a technology legend. He proved that excessive enthusiasm and excitement can lead to unimaginable achievement. Your road to superior performance requires the same dedication and insight.

If at first you don't succeed, destroy all the evidence that you tried.
If that is not possible, blame it on the person who just left the organization.
BW

A few thoughts from W. C. Fields

- *Don't borrow money from a bank without letting it know.*
- *You can fool half of the people half of the time and that's enough to make a living.*
- *Start every day with a smile and get it over with.*
- *Count your change before leaving the window.*
- *The best cure for insomnia is to get more sleep.*
- *I never met a kid I liked.*

Believe in tomorrow, but focus on today.

Bruce Patton

Be polite. Despite rumors to the contrary, good manners are always appropriate. On the other hand, bad manners are never welcomed or acceptable. Demonstrating hospitality and courtesy to friends, associates, and especially your family, is critical. Courtesy should always be an extension of your relationships. It also shows your mother raised you right.

Hubris is a killer.

Your approach to communications is a reflection of your professional demeanor and attention to detail. Regardless of the communications form, the objective is to inform the recipient of a particular subject, action, request or result.

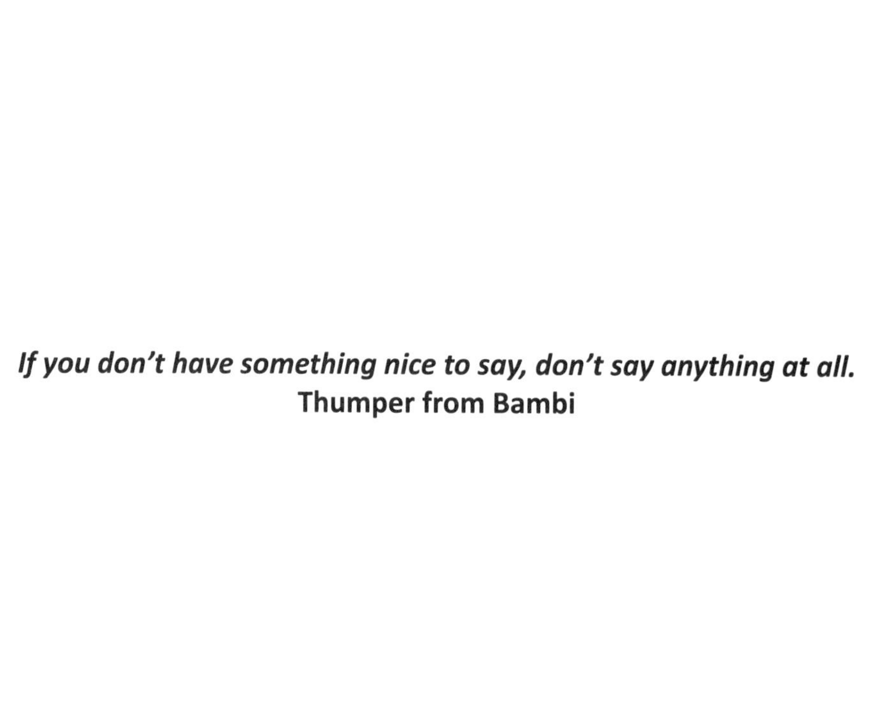

If you don't have something nice to say, don't say anything at all.
Thumper from Bambi

A survey conducted by the London School of Business concluded that only 10 percent of professionals are expert at getting things done in a highly efficient and effective manner. The study's conclusion was that the best way to be more productive is to simply make a commitment to be more productive.

In championship games you can't be timid.
Brian Kelly, Notre Dame Football coach

To be a superstar one must follow five simple rules: be prepared, be knowledgeable, be self-assured, be determined and be willing to provide high quality service."

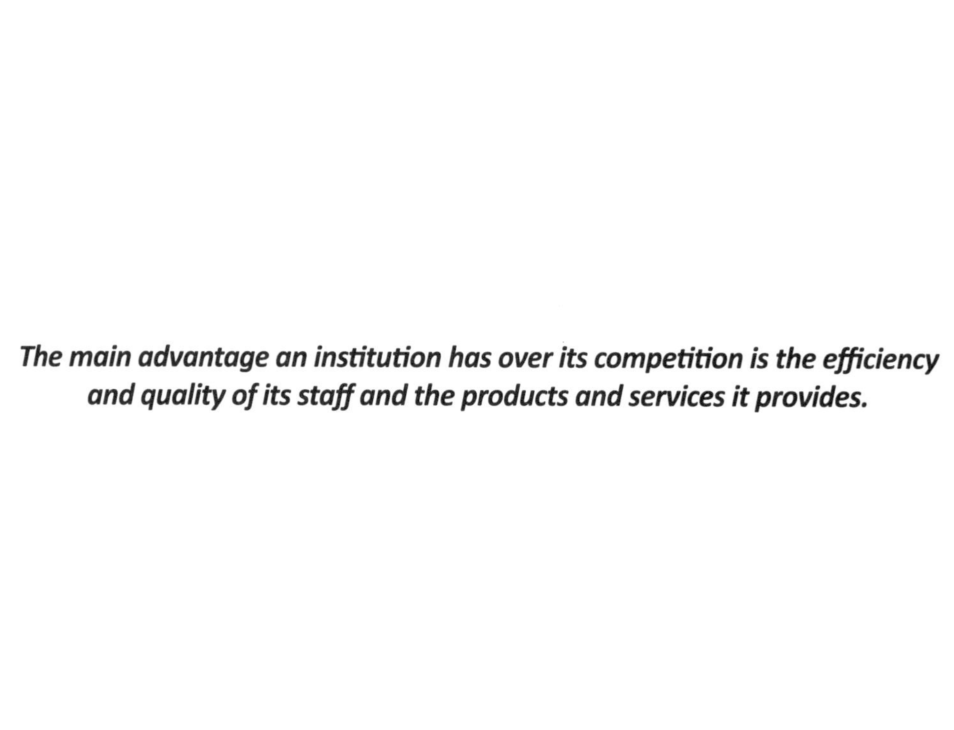

The main advantage an institution has over its competition is the efficiency and quality of its staff and the products and services it provides.

While counterintuitive, the customer is not always right. Some individuals and organizations are so demanding that maintaining a meaningful relationship may not be worth the time, effort or resources necessary to meet their expectations. In many organizations the customer comes second. This is often a winning strategy. It is alright to tell individuals that a relationship must be good for both participants. Include your expectations, not just what makes the other party happy. It will build a stronger, better relationship through mutual respect.

Sell the sizzle.

Individuals buy goods and services to make their lives better and enhance their image. A red convertible has never been purchased because the tires last forever. What sells a convertible is a sunny day with the top down and the wind in one's hair. Assure the clients with the features and benefits. Sell the clients by appealing to their emotions.

Sometimes you just have to belly up the bar and take a chance. We made some mistakes, but we also had the strength to work our way out.

Michael Dell

Michael Dell revolutionized direct-sales to consumers. He combined highly competitive prices with superior customer service and built an empire. His business principles include being completely honest, being straightforward with employees, taking responsibility for one's actions, making no excuses for actions gone astray, taking no victory laps, being a team member, building profits, increasing sales and eliminating underperforming ventures.

All the world's a stage, And all the men and women merely players.
William Shakespeare, *As You Like It*

In important meetings you want to control the environment. In comfortable surroundings, you gain an advantage. Your opportunities are also enhanced to project a positive image, act in a highly professional manner and be verbally persuasive. The strategy is to seamlessly combine appearance, atmosphere and behavior into a winning combination. The objective is to engage the listener in the process. The goal is to accomplish your objective.

There is no perfect solution.

The best crisis management plan employs a systematic approach. You identify the challenge, evaluate the circumstances and consider possible solutions. Then you determine the best course of action, implement the solution and provide the resources to resolve the problem. Once the plan of action is initiated, it is critical that you maintain leadership, accountability and transparency.

Anyone can identify the problem. Winners provide the solution.

Success is in the eye of the beholder, but you should understand that you will be compared to industry standards, your peers, management guidelines and your mother-in-law's expectations. It is important to know how to evaluate your performance while keeping score. Be realistic in your expectations. Understand that learning is a process, not an event.

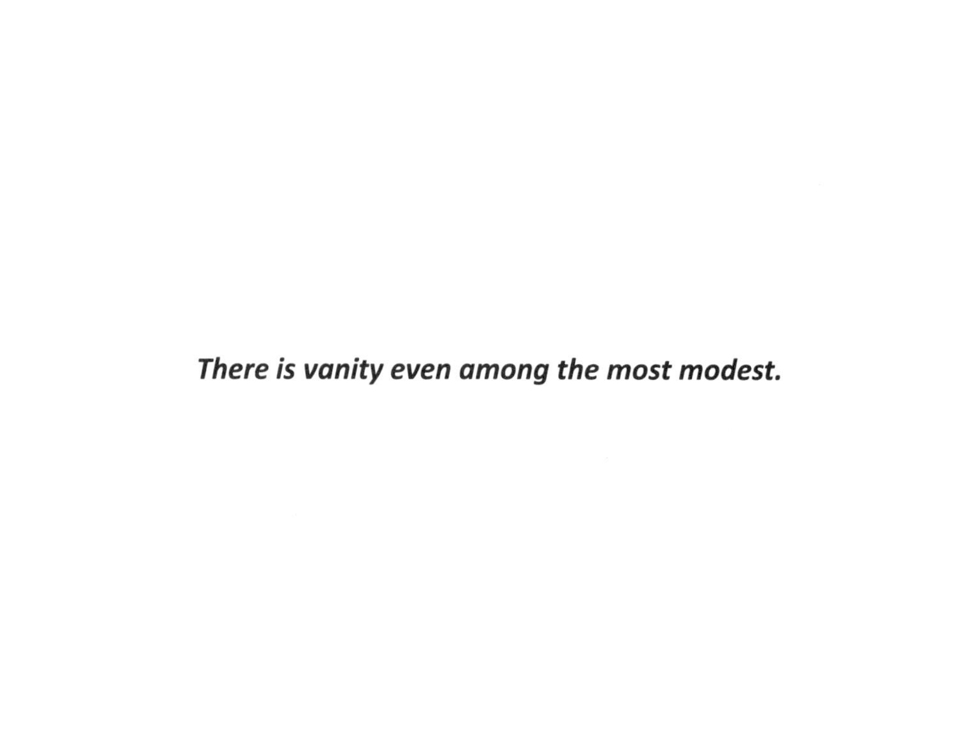

There is vanity even among the most modest.

Be formal. I have never experienced an awkward moment when greeting someone in a formal manner, i.e. Mister, Ms., Doctor or Sir. I have seen resentment shown by mature individuals or senior management personnel being addressed in an informal manner by a less titled associate or a member of a younger generation. Be smart, be formal, be mannerly. Brashness and perceived lack of respect is often a deal breaker.

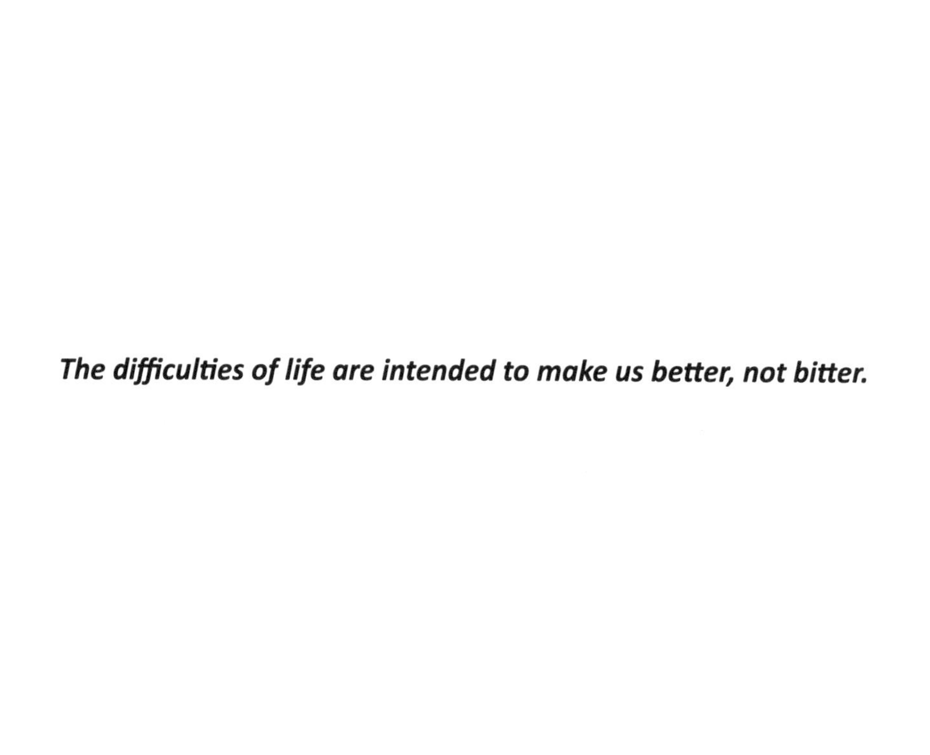

The difficulties of life are intended to make us better, not bitter.

Be sensitive to lifestyle and cultural differences. It's a new world. Respect for others is an absolute for both the business environment and your personal relationships. Civility and courtesy are not optional. It is not important that you agree with, or approve of, certain policies, procedures, lifestyles or personal beliefs. What is essential is that you respect the differences.

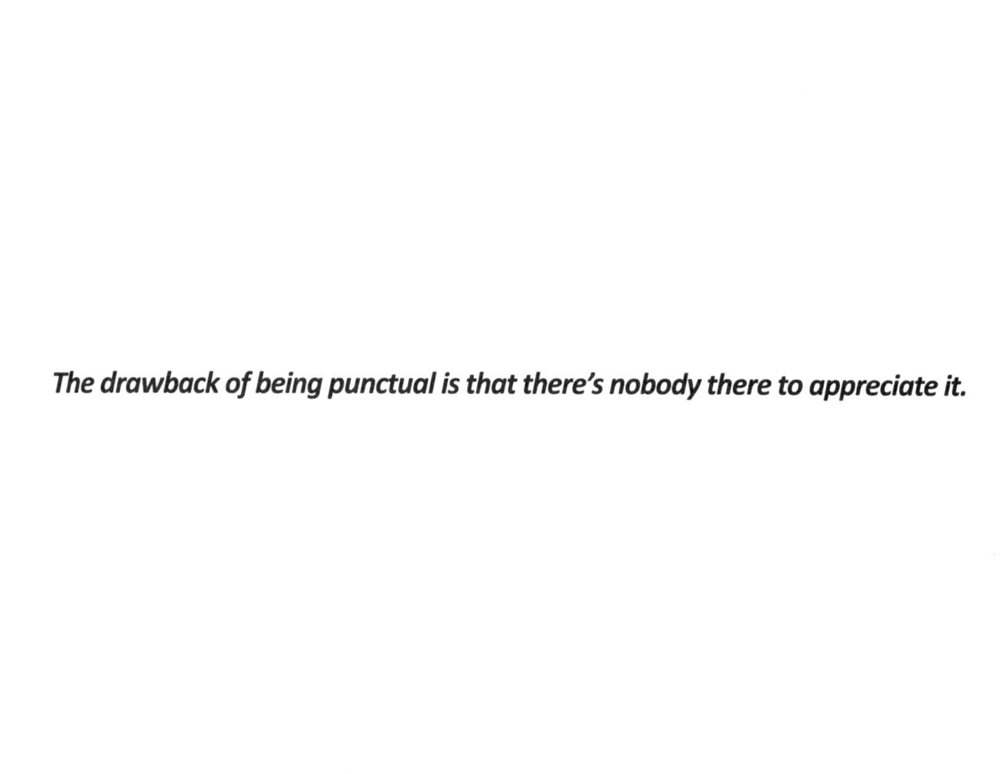

The drawback of being punctual is that there's nobody there to appreciate it.

Be early for business meetings and conferences. It's a senior executive habit. Pre-meeting time is a great opportunity to meet informally with senior executives, clients, peers and subordinates. Be assured people take note of early arrivals. The exception is a cocktail party or reception. A moderately late arrival is usually acceptable and, in many instances, accepted protocol.

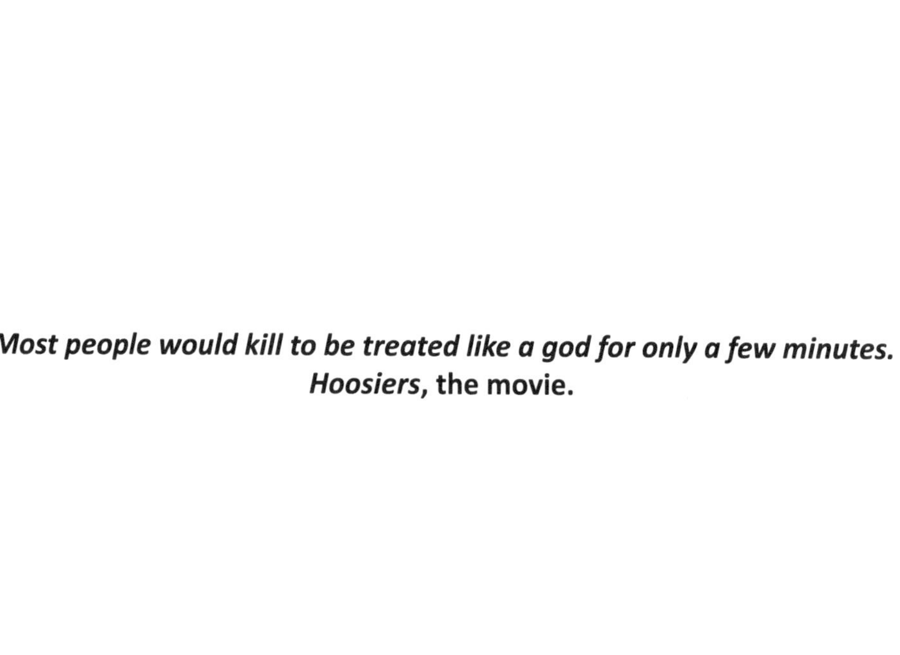

Most people would kill to be treated like a god for only a few minutes.

Hoosiers, the movie.

Develop a system of contact follow-up for your personal relationships and career endeavors. This is not just a case of organization; but a case of positive image. How many times have individuals simply not returned a call? It is the single biggest complaint of willing buyers and your mother. When you return calls promptly you are among a unique group. You set yourself apart. In relationships returning calls is polite. In business dealings returning calls is essential.

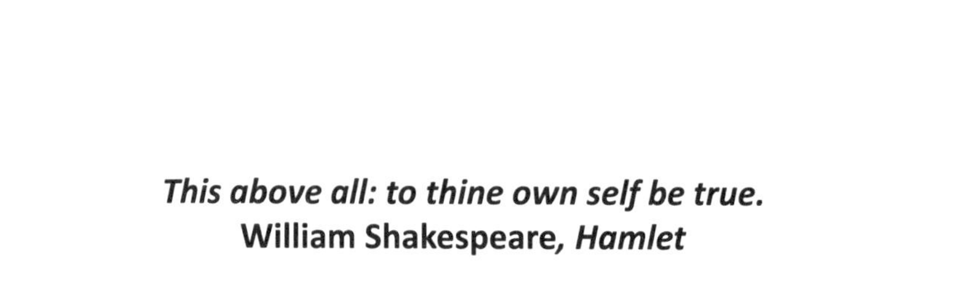

This above all: to thine own self be true.
William Shakespeare, *Hamlet*

Believe in a higher good. Whether it's charity, church, community or family or all the above, make it a point to remember that it's not about you. However, it is reasonable to be successful, healthy and self-confident. In fact it can be selfless. It allows you to share the wealth and contribute to positive acts. Everyone likes and admires a generous winner. It's that image thing again.

Being a quality person is not an objective, it is a way of living your life to the fullest.

Learn to say no. Never accept an assignment or volunteer for an activity unless you can devote the time necessary to do it well. Both business and civic duties should be approached in a highly professional manner. Your participation in the activities directly reflects on your professionalism, standing at the office and reputation in the community.

Do not kill the messenger. Keep communications open. Being well informed is the key to your relationships. Early awareness makes problem solving easier.

Listen to the people who are important to you. Most people talk too much. Become a better listener. Confirm your understanding to the individual with whom you are speaking. You will be clear on the message and be able to better support the individual. You will also gain the confidence of the person and be perceived as a person who understands and cares. This is particularly true of family members.

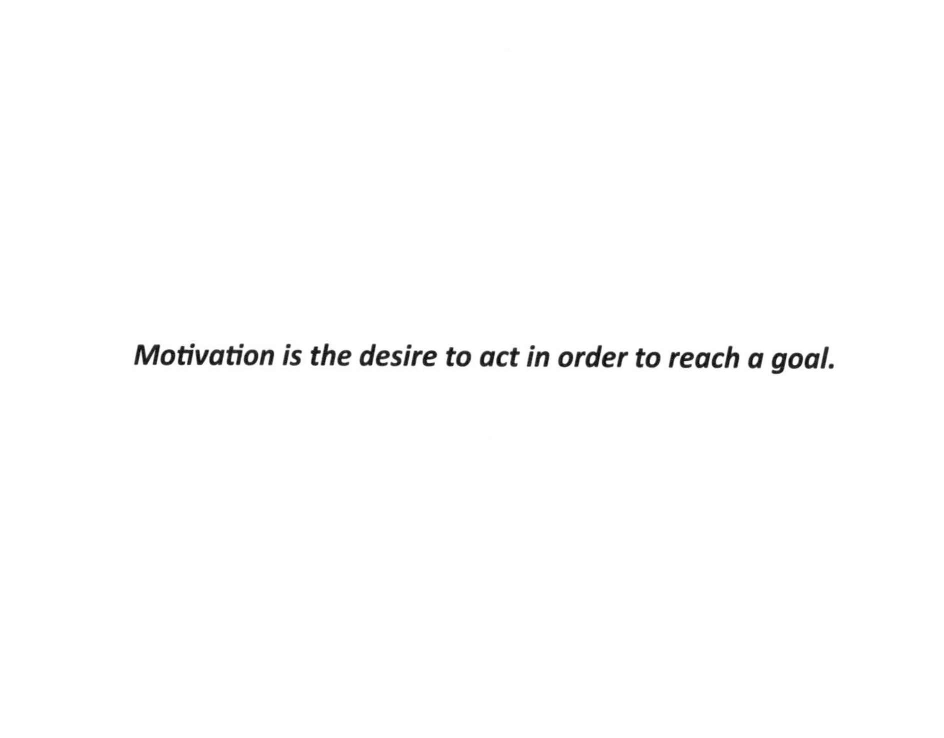
Motivation is the desire to act in order to reach a goal.

Credibility is important. Universities, colleges, junior colleges and community education centers seek qualified instructors to teach both college level and continuing education courses. The income from the endeavor is modest. However, presenting yourself as a highly qualified expert to the community will enhance your image, introduce you to an influential segment of the community and add an impressive line on your resume.

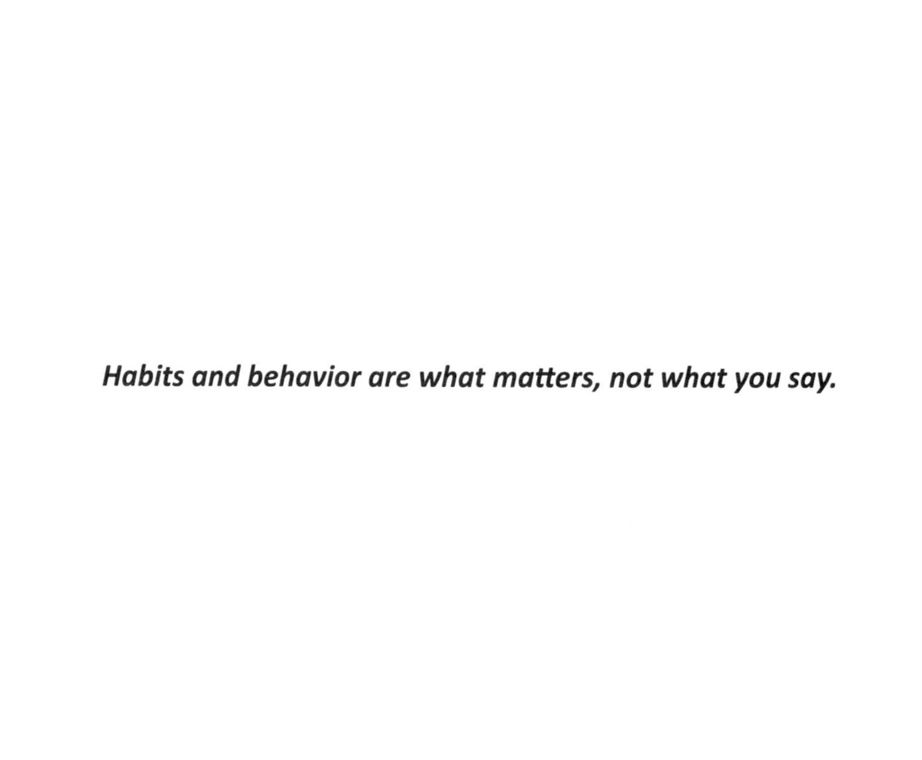

Habits and behavior are what matters, not what you say.

Beat your best performance. Successful highly acclaimed winners, no matter what their talent, strive to become even more proficient. Great actors, salespersons, athletes, attorneys and artists continually practice their craft. Improvement is a never ending quest for success and the goal of professionals.

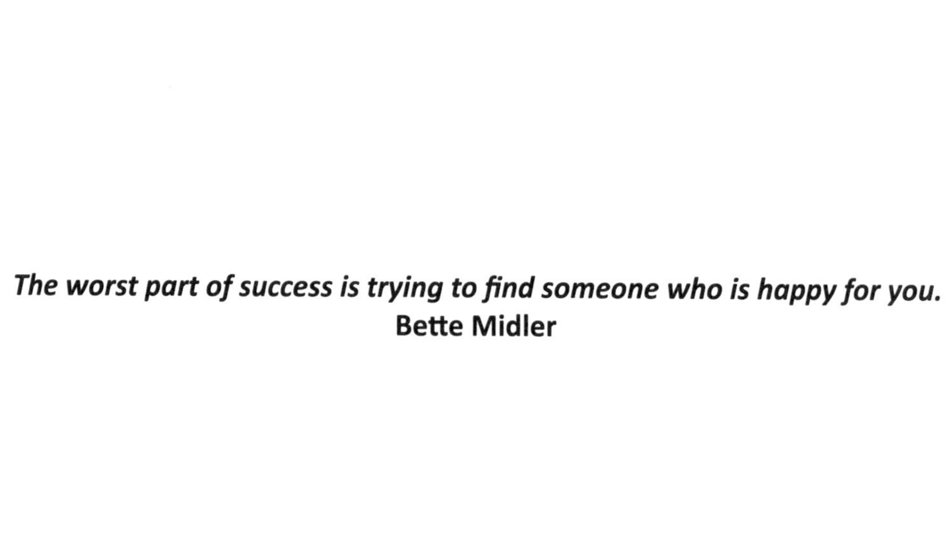

The worst part of success is trying to find someone who is happy for you.

Bette Midler

The best laid plans for the fast track to success are often derailed by a milk-train schedule. Choosing the slow career train is an easy route to a lifestyle that flourishes among the ordinary. It offers a route to mediocrity and the status of “I could have been a contender.” Now is the time to catch the express. Improve your life and advance your career. How? Plan, think, take charge and execute.

Talk doesn't cook rice.

Chinese Proverb

Warren Buffett has a five point strategy for investing. The five points can also be a life lesson for success.

- Almost doesn’t count.
- Believe in your best ideas.
- Be true to your style.
- Be open to change.
- Be patient - wait for your pitch.

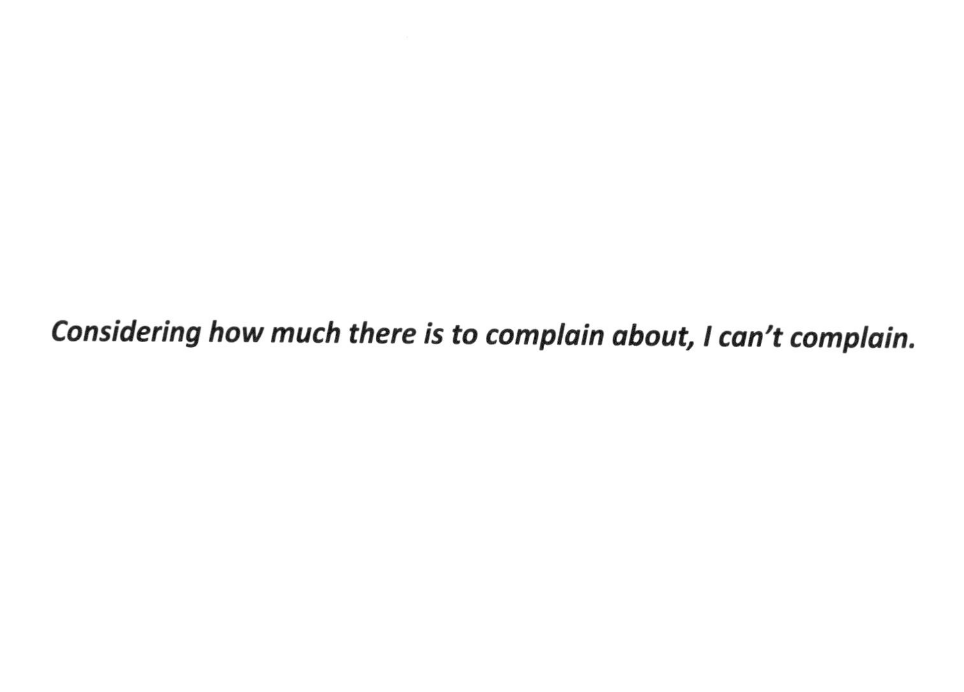

Considering how much there is to complain about, I can't complain.

Know the difference between contributing and complaining. Management is "looking for solutions, not problems." Present challenges to associates in a realistic and accurate manner. Outline the importance, urgency, advantages and consequences. Don't editorialize. Discuss potential solutions. Bottom line? Present a complete and accurate report.

If you tell the truth, you don't have to remember anything.

Mark Twain

Be brief. The best advice for professionals making a presentation is to be brief, be good and be gone. Also be unhurried, courteous, efficient and friendly, but be brief. This is also true for telephone calls, e-mails and personal visits.

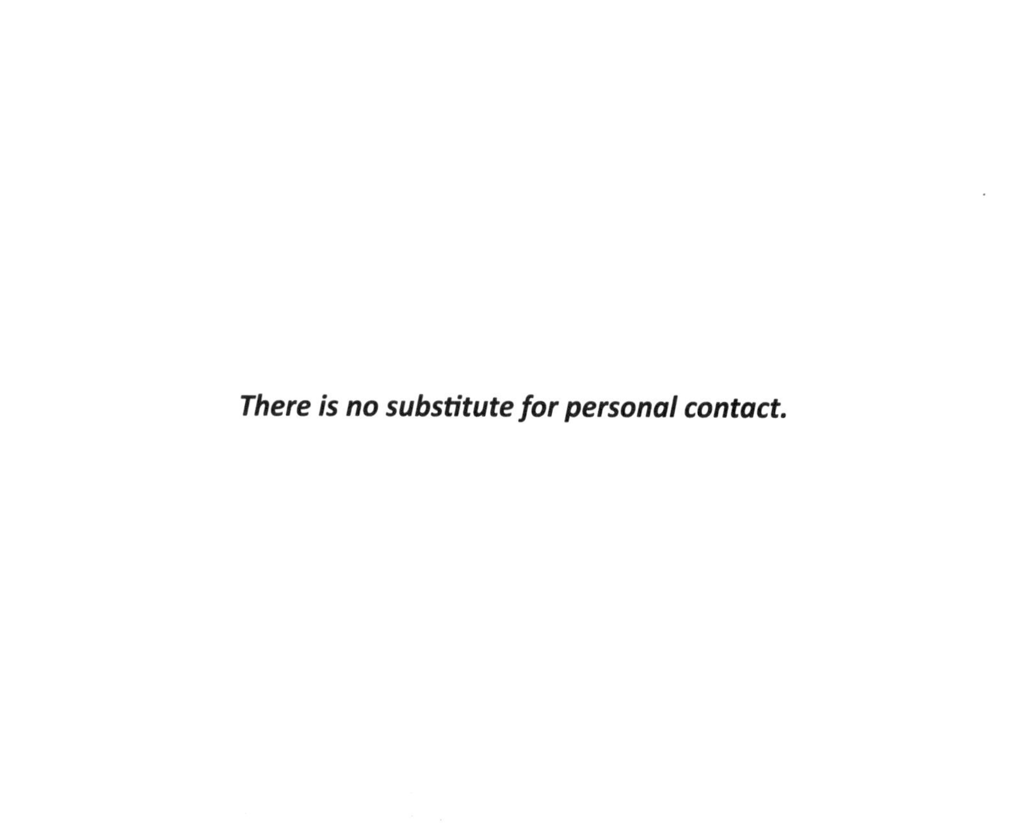

There is no substitute for personal contact.

Unless absolutely necessary, do not screen calls. It's about both image and efficiency. Nothing is more frustrating than having a telephone gate keeper interrogate a caller to determine if the caller is worthy of an audience with their senior associate. If you answer calls immediately, taking messages and returning calls are eliminated. Most important, you project a professional image.

Plan for what is difficult when it is easy. Do what is great while it is small.

Sun Tzu, *The Art of War*

Airline pilots have a check-list they complete before each flight, regardless of how experienced the pilot, how brief the flight, or how big the aircraft. Professionals can be more successful by maintaining the same strategy.

A thousand words will not leave so deep an impression as one good deed.
Henrik Isben

Hackneyed versions of homespun chestnuts are often stated, primarily because they are true. Your lesson for the day, grasshopper, is, "You will never have a second opportunity to make a good first impression."

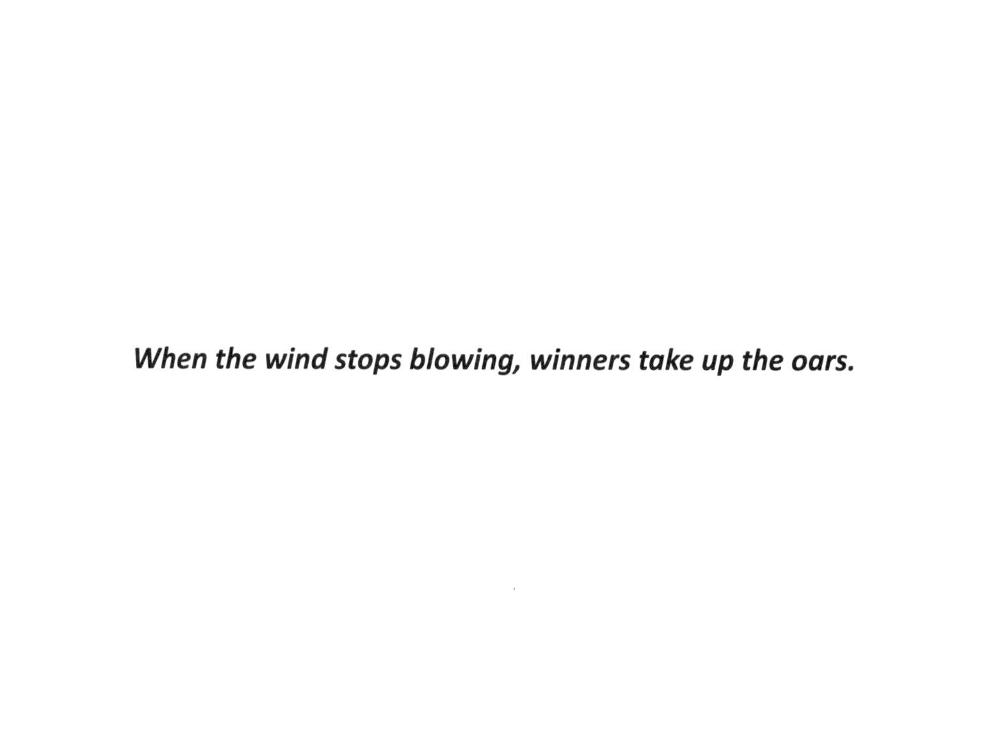

When the wind stops blowing, winners take up the oars.

A winning attitude will enhance your performance. Ask yourself four questions. What is a winning attitude? Do I have a winning attitude? Do I display a winning attitude? Am I willing to commit to being a winner?

Seven times fall, stand up eight.

Japanese Proverb

Set high goals and objectives. You can be one of the most successful people in your profession simply by having a clear understanding of what it takes to win. To paraphrase many, "90 percent of winning is just showing up." Did I mention also be on time?

Very little is needed to make a happy life; it is all within yourself, in your way of thinking.

Marcus Aurelius

Learn a new skill. The major benefit is mastering a skill that is enjoyable and allows you to relax. It provides a sense of accomplishment. For quick and fun results, try juggling. A suggestion: become proficient with the rubber balls before juggling the chain saws.

Our greatest weakness lies in giving up. The most certain way to succeed is always to try and to take more time.

Thomas Edison

Refuse to lose. Be highly motivated to succeed. Stress that failure is not an option. Realize that most "things" are not that important. A great skill is to know the difference. A compromise, if fair and equitable, is a win for everyone. Regardless, always be cordial. That is always a winning strategy.

The Ben Franklin Method: Draw a line down the middle. Put pros to the left and cons to the right.

Write it down. On a single page, outline your personal and professional attributes. Then list the traits and skills you want to improve. Write a personal strategy combining your strengths with your goals and objectives. Determine the effort and resources to make your "dream" resume become a reality. Make it happen.

You are never too old to set another goal or to dream a new dream.

C. S. Lewis

How do you get there from here? The wonderful thing about successful individuals is that they are creative, determined and ambitious. The question is how successful do you want to be? The way to find out is to determine what you want to do, have the utmost faith that you can do it, and plan your final destination with milestones along the way.

Commitment is an act, not a word.

Jean-Paul Sartre

Do something, even if it is wrong. There are two phases to making important decisions: evaluation and execution. Remember the other choice is to do nothing. Once the decision is made to move forward, make a 100% commitment to its execution. It's a done deal; case closed. What usually happens is that all will go well. If not, the results will still be better than that of vacillation, inaction and indecision.

The best time to ask for a referral
is when you have done a good job for someone.

Always ask for referrals. Top professionals always ask for referrals, that's why they are outstanding performers. If pursued, a high percentage of referrals will close. While hard to believe, most qualified referrals received are never contacted by the person receiving the referral. Talk about leaving money on the table.

ATTITUDE

Sign in FSU locker room

Anticipate client objections. Before making a buying decision, clients interested in your products and services will seek clarification. Develop factual, informative and completely accurate responses to regularly asked client questions. Stress benefits but don't get consumed in the minutiae of performance or expectations. Mastering the art of answering questions for clarification will dramatically increase your effectiveness. Remember, questions are almost always inquiries seeking clarification, not true objections.

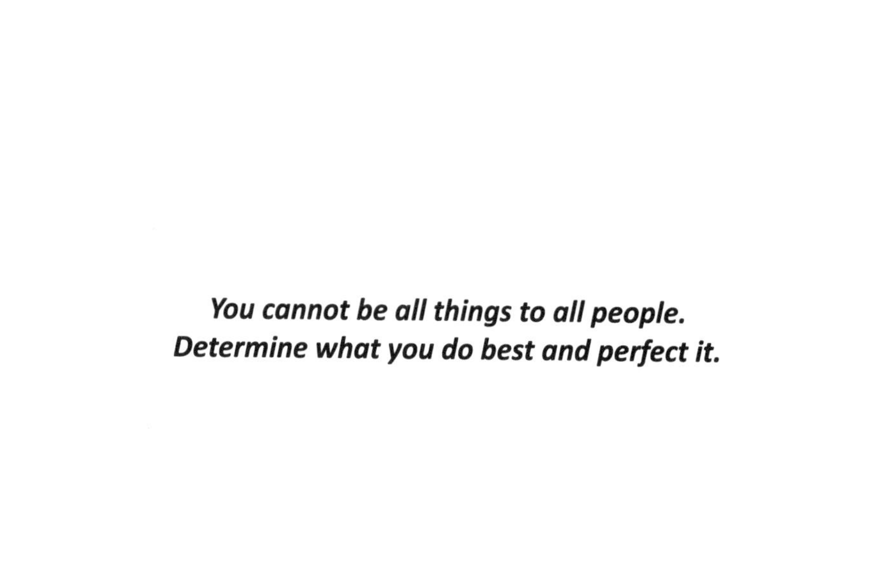

You cannot be all things to all people.
Determine what you do best and perfect it.

Find a niche in the marketplace. Position yourself in a clearly defined role and you will be perceived as an expert. More importantly, you will be treated with respect. Marketing yourself is a necessity, not an option. Always be pro-active. Find vendors who will support your efforts. While often difficult to separate yourself with unique products, you can easily separate yourself with unique, professional, efficient, sky-box customer service. Use FedEx as your model.

You can't help everyone, but everyone can help someone.

Ronald Reagan

To the surprise of many, one's success does not depend on time spent in the office. It is more about what you do when you are at the office. Individuals who work a 60 to 80 hour week will be well served to examine their priorities, work habits and effectiveness. Road warriors, young corporate attorneys and Wall Street types get a pass on the evaluation. An examination for time management is useful for all groups. One absolute: on-time arrival is a prerequisite for success, no exceptions.

There is little competition if you are prepared, willing to hustle and always work hard.

Stay in touch with your competition. As a sales manager, sales person, administrator or line manager there are advantages to knowing how your industry operates and who the "players" are. Industry meetings are a good source for current information. So is lunch with a competitor. There are few trade secrets. Successful individuals are almost always willing to share ideas. All participants will benefit.

If they did it in the past, they will do it in the future.

BW

Managers who have the most success building and maintaining a top-tier team are those who thoroughly “screen” applicants. 90 percent of the hiring success is the initial selection process. Experience is a good indicator. If a person has been successful in the past, given the right opportunity, they will be successful in the future. Resist the temptation to just “fill the spot” quickly. An inappropriate hire will cost you more in aggravation than an empty chair.

Adventure is just bad planning.
Ronald Amundsen

“Things” do not always go well. Like your brother-in-law on the couch, you just want the problem to go away but wishing so is not a strategy. Pre-planning will solve problems more quickly and reduce the consequences. Take affirmative action. That’s how smart businesses survive. Have strategies that are readily available. Continue to refine a grand strategy (vision statement) that quantifies your objectives. The worst question to ask is “what do we do now?” Highly successful people already know the answer.

Some people succeed because they are destined to, but most people succeed because they are determined to.

Bruce's 10 plus three strategies to immediately enhance your image:

Be encouraging, constructive and optimistic
Show humility (you don't have to mean it)
Dress well (dressed, pressed and stylish)
Make others the center of attention
Return ALL calls in a timely manner
Define your primary objective
Design your emails carefully
Never lose your temper
Self manage well
Never complain
Be on time
Practice
Listen

Act like you have been there before.
Coach Tom Landry, Dallas Cowboys

Be confident enough to be humble. One will earn respect by reacting modestly to success. Why professional athletes do an end zone dance defies logic for individuals seeking a positive image. Young fans may be impressed but most adults' reaction is "give me a break." The person who brags about possessions, compensation, family and/or successes is doing an end zone dance. It's all about insecurity. The more successful, the less accomplishments should be mentioned (everyone already knows).

To disagree, one doesn't have to be disagreeable.

Barry Goldwater

When someone tells you it can't do something, it is often because they are afraid you will. When it is too hard, it usually isn't too hard. Just break it down into smaller bites.

The greater the mystery surrounding you,
the greater the respect shown to you.
BW

Enhance your professional image by not discussing personal matters of substance with your associates or clients. The more individuals know about your personal life, the more likely you are to diminish the aura of your accomplishments and credentials. Too much information dilutes the focus of the relationship. It will also take the shine off the apple.

Compromise is the best and cheapest lawyer.

Robert Lewis Stevenson

Be willing to compromise. Decide which principles are important to you. Support them appropriately. Not all strategies and ideas are critical or even important, at least to you. Be willing to support matters that are important to others but have no consequential affect on your strategies. You will be viewed as a reasonable team player. Remember, you will need the concurrence of others on "things" that really do matter to you.

You are never fully dressed without a smile.
Martin Charnin

Personal dress is important but so is your "stuff." Making a positive impression includes all your tools of the trade. Your vehicle should be shiny and clean. Your computer bag should be fashionable. A stylish pen is critical. Your watch? What can I say? Plastic is not cool, Leroy. Be understated but elegant with all your accessories. You want to be the coolest dude in the room.

Respect is what we owe; love is what we give.

Phillip James Bailey

Being respectful is an adjunct to courteousness. Never use risqué humor or profanity. Leave the off-color remarks to the comedians. Practice the skill of euphemistic remarks. Softer descriptions make the message clear while the messenger is considered polite and cordial. As an example, the statement "Bless his little heart" is a much softer way of saying a person is dumb as a rock.

I am not a crook!
President Richard M. Nixon

Get a difficult issue out front before it "blows up." Immediately address the issue in an honest manner. By being straightforward you control the circumstances, the information and reduce the exposure. You also lessen the immediate damage. Remember a misrepresentation of the facts is usually more serious than the initial problem. The worst response is to attempt a cover up. However, if you think the matter might just go away, you may want to keep your mouth shut for a few days to see what happens.

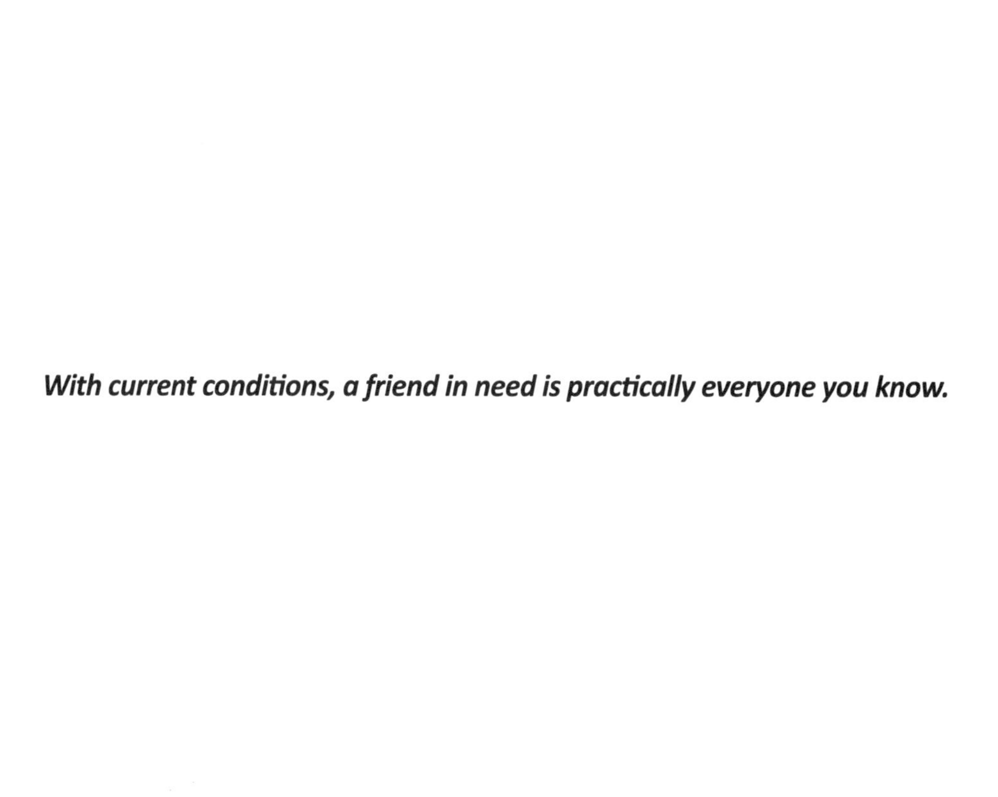

With current conditions, a friend in need is practically everyone you know.

Loyalty and true friendship have become less prevalent. My dad always said "never trade an old friend for a new friend." It's still good advice but be realistic in your expectations. Friends are there through thick and thin, are not judgmental, maintain trust, keep secrets and practice discretion. Friends are for life. Friendly relations are usually at work. You are lucky if your true friends are counted on more than one hand.

Well done is always better than well said.

Benjamin Franklin

A trait that is often overlooked that complements a professional image is assuming responsibility. Are you dedicated to performing well? Are you accountable? Are you responsible for your actions? In other words are you a team member? If so, you are a winner and you will be recognized as such.

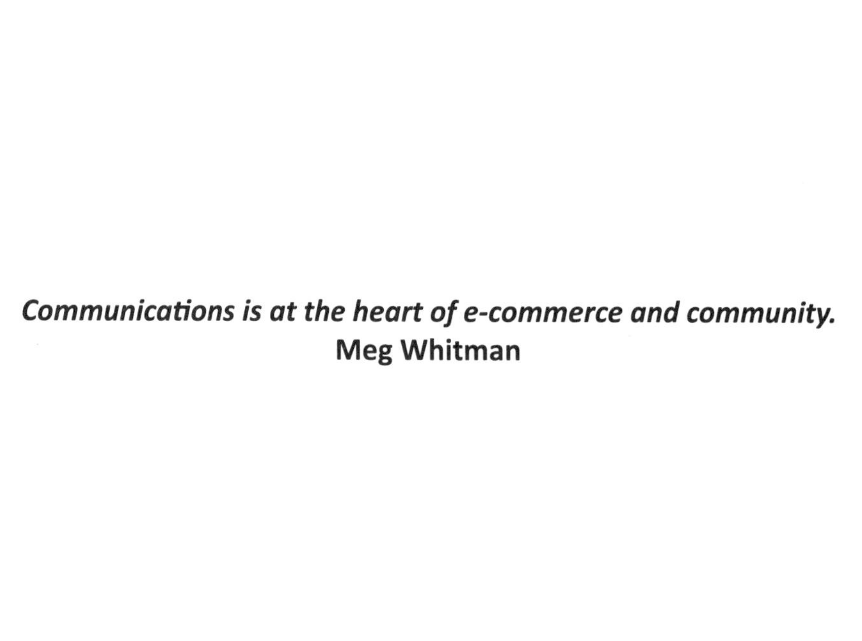

Communications is at the heart of e-commerce and community.
Meg Whitman

Build a positive image by staying in touch. Maintain contact with individuals you see less often. The contacts should always be pleasant. The encounters provide an opportunity to acknowledge the relationship, particularly in cases of congratulations, celebrations, contributions and accomplishments. Always make the conversation about them. The less you talk, the smarter you look!

Action is eloquence.
William Shakespeare, *Coriolanus*

The hand written note makes a good impression simply because the note is traditional. In today's world a personal note is fast becoming unique. First tip: have presentable handwriting. Second tip: develop a distinctive signature. Third tip: use a wide tip pin. Fourth tip: use personalized note cards.

Be amusing, never tell unkind stories; above all, never tell long ones.

Benjamin Disraeli

A few thoughts from **Mark Twain**

- As always, a deal that sounds too good to be true probably is.
- Make money and the whole world will conspire to call you a gentleman.
- It is the difference of opinion that makes horse-races.
- For business reasons, I must preserve the outward signs of sanity.
- Honesty is the best policy - when there is money in it.

Education gives you knowledge. Street smarts give you an edge.
Money gives you choices.

There is always room for improvement. Seek ways to enhance your image. Do it gradually. Sudden, drastic changes may actually create a sense of uncertainty and doubt among your acquaintances. Eliminate the notion that there is a right or wrong image. Realize that there is an appropriate positive image for your professional and personal life.

Colors, like features, follow the changes of the emotions.
Pablo Pisacco

Color combinations can project a positive image. Blue projects calmness. Gray represents a culture choice of affluence and influence. Black and white combined signals upper class. Your color selections should reflect the image you seek. Artists, fashion designers, techies and food servers, among others, are examples of individuals who dress to project a particular, and hopefully unique, image by wearing bright colors, high fashion and other identifying "uniforms." The style depends on the image you seek.

Leadership is about taking responsibility, not making excuses.

Mitt Romney

Be a responsible citizen. Contribute to scholarship funds, civic organizations and other charities. Even modest donations are appreciated. Being known as an individual who cares has great public relations benefits. Being generous gives you a good feeling about yourself. Participation is relatively inexpensive and is always noticed.

A warm smile and a gracious manner will destroy an adversary more quickly than any weapon.

BW

Speak to everyone. Individuals always appreciate the recognition and the fact you took the time to say hello. Make sure you always include the occasional individual with whom you share a less than cordial relationship. You appear to be gracious and magnanimous. The fun part is that the recipient of your kindness can't "figure" you out, a winning moment.

Some are born great, some achieve greatness and some hire a public relations firm.

Be your own public relations firm. Become a volunteer spokesperson for a public interest group or charity. Present your program to the local media. Speak at business and civic clubs about your cause. You gain from the exposure, are recognized as a community leader, and, most important, serve a worthy cause.

There is no greater charisma than sincerity and honest intent.

BW

Some happy thoughts from (the not very famous) **Bruce Wells**

Beware of the vegan whose favorite restaurant is a steak house.

I only know two songs on the banjo; one is You Are My Sunshine and the other one isn't.

As a hunter I have never been bitten by a snake. Wall Street is another matter. Their snakes wear suits.

Informing an audience will get you applause. Entertaining an audience will get you cheers.

The more I express my opinions the fewer friends who will go to lunch with me.

If all else fails, wrap yourself in the flag.

George Clooney personifies style and grace.

Always buy the first round. They never get any cheaper.

BW

There are two circumstances that can "absolutely" get you fired or reprimanded. One is a Christmas party or other company function where alcohol is served. The other is your expense account. Without exception, do not fiddle at one or fiddle with the other. While not a popular approach, believe me when I tell you that a no alcohol consumption policy at a company function is strategic to your career. Your approach to expenses speaks to your honesty and integrity. Be smart.

The purpose of life is to serve and show compassion.
It is also a way to make the sale.

"The best sales people have the ability to understand where someone else is coming from, the drive to bring others around to their point of view, the desire to come through for others, the conscientiousness to complete projects and the ability to bounce back from rejection." **Herbert M. Greenberg**, CEO of Caliper

A prospect is a prospect only when they are willing to listen, willing to buy and willing to spend the money.

Prospecting is a process of elimination. The steps are simple; the execution is another matter. The biggest time saver and career builder is identifying qualified prospects. Determine who can benefit from your products and/or services and solicit them. It is not a popularity contest. You are looking to be a top producer, not the most popular person at the prom.

Play Like a Champion Today.

Sign in the Notre Dame locker room

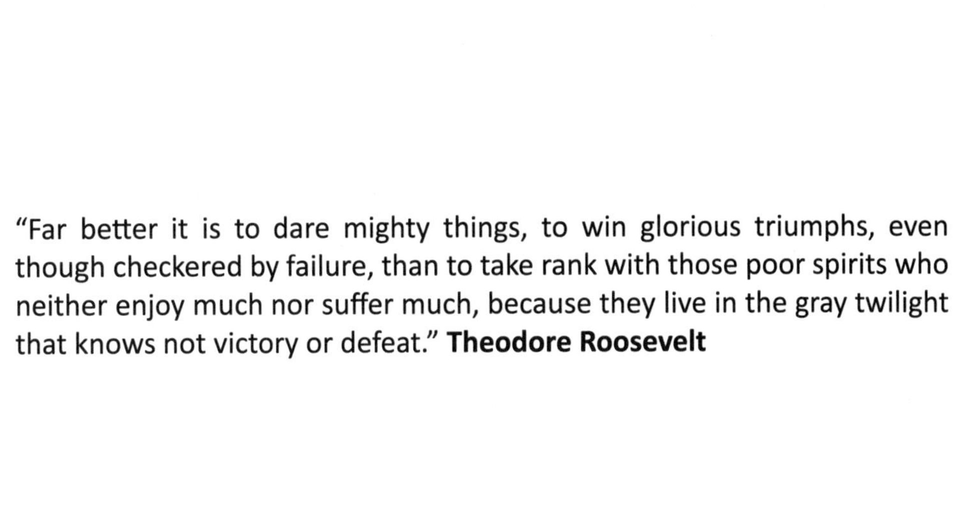

"Far better it is to dare mighty things, to win glorious triumphs, even though checkered by failure, than to take rank with those poor spirits who neither enjoy much nor suffer much, because they live in the gray twilight that knows not victory or defeat." **Theodore Roosevelt**

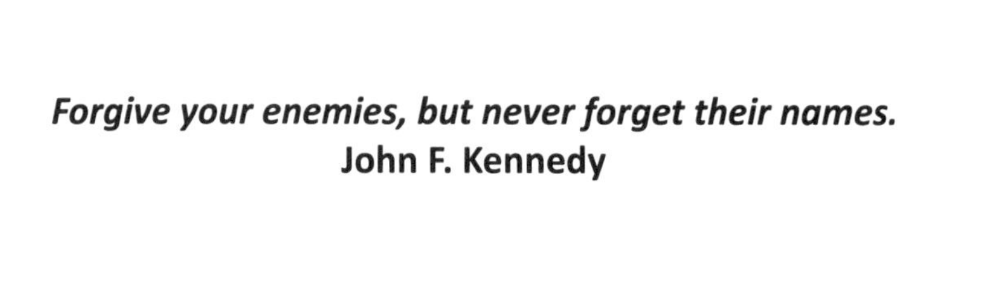

Forgive your enemies, but never forget their names.
John F. Kennedy

Remember names. Clients are easy. Remembering support personnel names requires more concentration and effort. When visiting a client's facilities, spend a few minutes with their support employees. Address them by name. If you don't know their names, ask. Folks always appreciate that you care enough to know them as individuals. Remember, support personnel often influence buying decisions. (Write down the names and use the list for reference when you visit, an easy solution.)

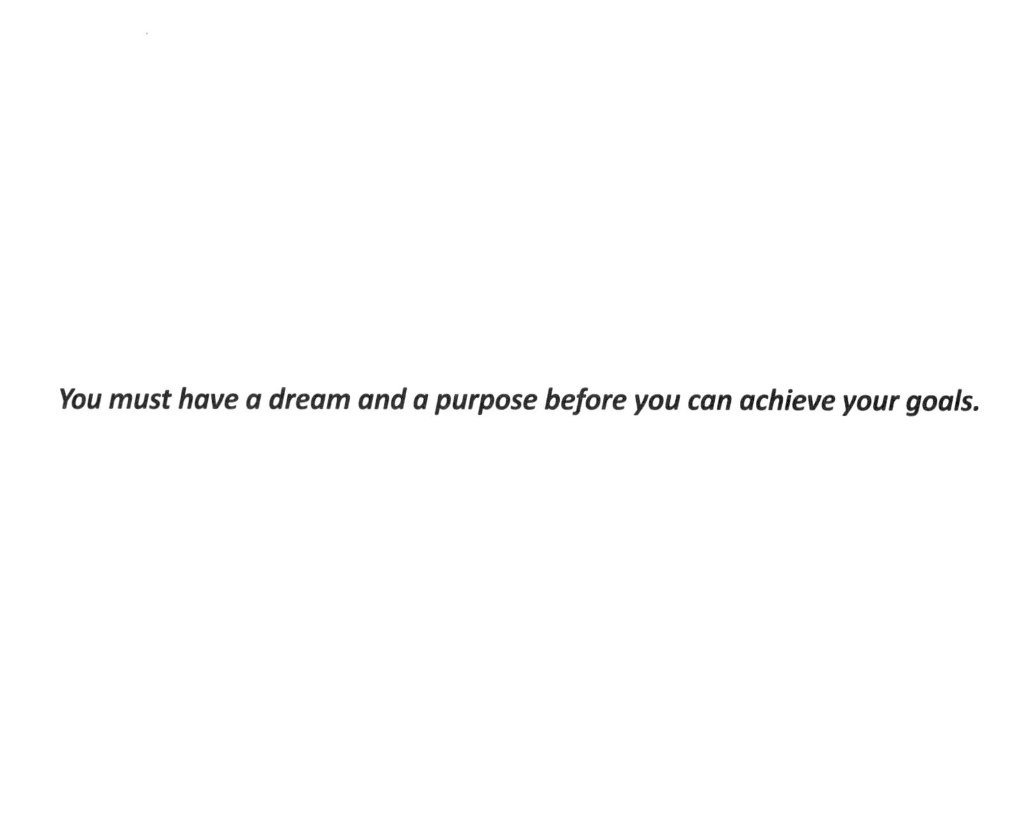
You must have a dream and a purpose before you can achieve your goals.

Think big. Solicit prospects and clients who will do meaningful business. Many important clients are already in your "book". New accounts require more development and attention. They are essential to maintaining your production level. Big tickets are great but elephant (big) sales require more effort and more attention to detail. You will also need modest sales to pay bills. Elephant sales buy cars.

The worst case seldom happens, and then only once.

BW

What is the worst case? It is a simple question and a dynamic planning tool. Actions have consequences. Before acting ask, “What happens if this thing blows up? What will be the consequences?” If the results could be catastrophic, your approach may not be a good idea regardless of the possible gains.

Commitment is a wonderful thing. I think a number of my family members should be committed.

BW

Learn to commit. One of the most admired qualities in a successful relationship, business or personal, is tenacity. Meet challenges along the road to success with a professional, upbeat and resolute attitude. Determination is the main ingredient to accomplishment.

Compassion is the first step to earning respect.

Positive coaching and positive reinforcement boost performance. So does praise for a job well done. Always commend employees for showing initiative and enhancing their job performance.

An ounce of practice is worth a ton of preaching.

Mahatma Gandhi

Practice regulation persuasion. Present compliance policies in an upbeat and objective manner. Explain why certain policies are essential. Rules violations can create significant issues. This is particularly important in the banking, insurance, real estate, mortgage, asset management, medical, legal and accounting industries. You are doing your employees a favor. Keep copious notes. We live in a society where many individuals are looking for someone to blame.

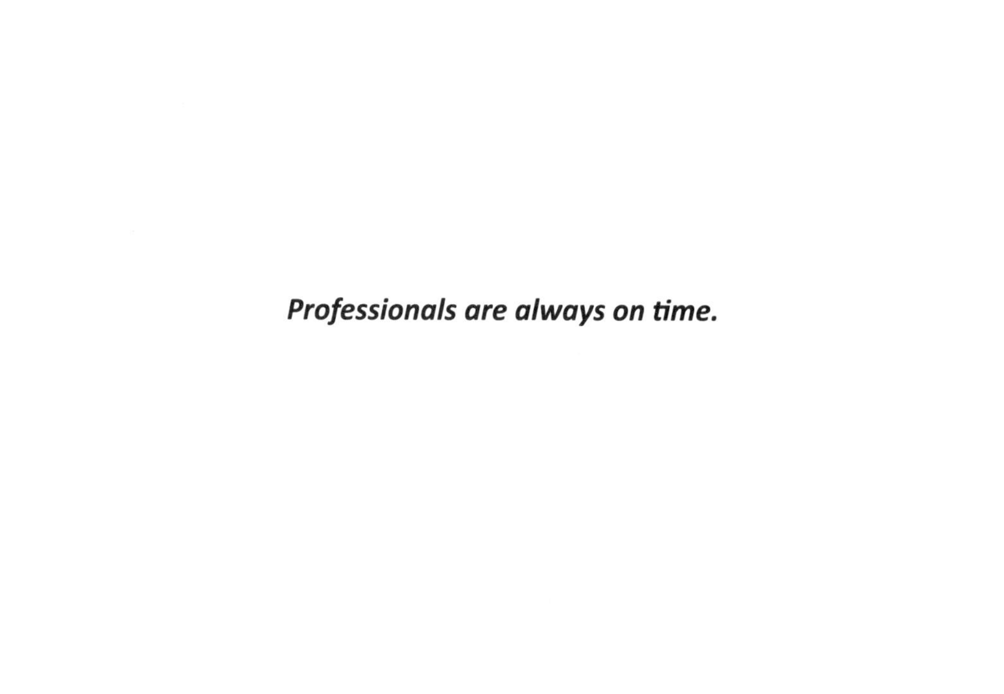

Professionals are always on time.

Work by appointment. Meeting clients in a planned and structured environment will maximize your efforts. Providing a professional approach will increase your credibility and stature. Reconfirm appointments the day before the scheduled meeting. Another call the day of the appointment is appropriate for new clients. The approach will dramatically decrease your "no-shows."

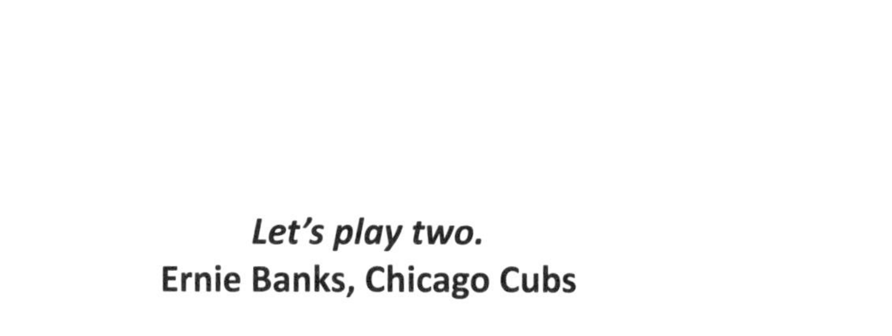

Let's play two.

Ernie Banks, Chicago Cubs

Come ready to play. Great athletes are successful because they are prepared. They come to play every day. Every time at bat is an opportunity to excel. In business it means having extensive knowledge about your products, services, customers, employees and competitors. The knowledge will enhance your execution skills.

I know nothing.

Sergeant Schultz

Focus on your goals. Ninety percent of water cooler conversations (do water coolers really still exist?) are rumors and speculation. Eliminate unnecessary encounters by not listening or giving credibility to the information. Don't participate in gossip. Stay busy building your career. Folks will get the message quickly that you are all business.

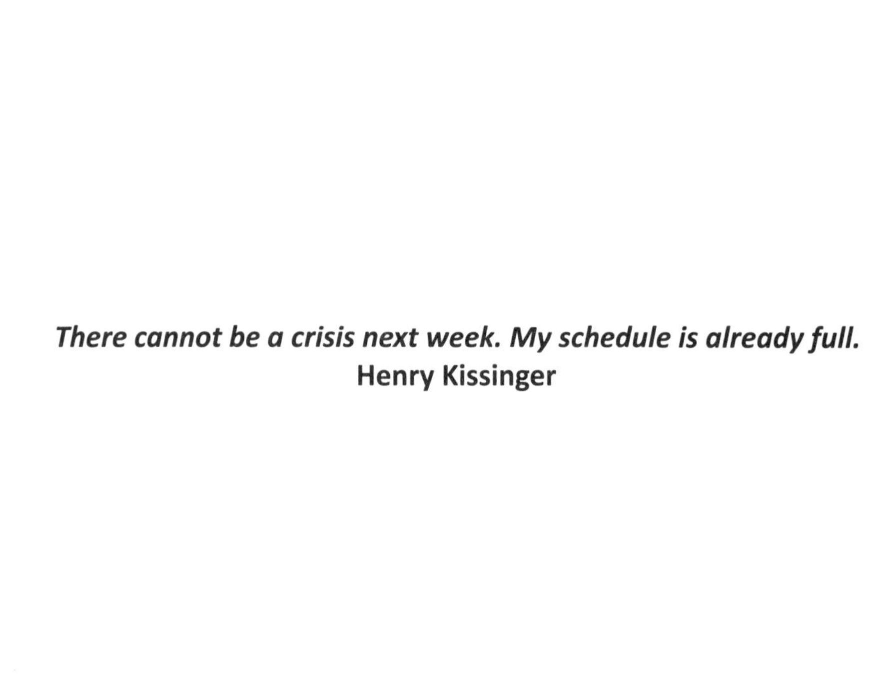

There cannot be a crisis next week. My schedule is already full.

Henry Kissinger

Have a "Plan B." What will you do if the highest and best use of your time is not possible? Be prepared. Appointments cancel, computers go down, transportation plans are interrupted, bags are lost, support personnel get sick and Power Point presentations and handouts don't arrive at the hotel. Since it's all show business, go on with the show, remembering that tomorrow is just a day away.

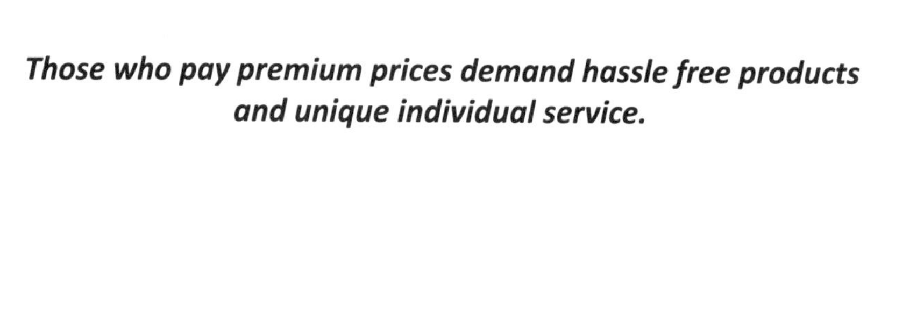

Those who pay premium prices demand hassle free products and unique individual service.

Bring a sky box mentality to your customer relations. In a highly competitive environment aggressive business marketing strategies are not only acceptable, but appropriate. Provide promotions that deliver value in ways that are superior to your competition.

Quality in a product or service is not what you put into it,
it is what the client or customer gets out of it.
Peter Drucker

The primary differences in selling upscale products and services as compared to commonplace products is quality, superior customer service and perceived value. Of the three, the most critical is quality service. It is assumed that you have selected quality products and that you are associated with a respected organization.

Manners are one of the greatest engines of influence ever given to man.

Mary Wilson Little

After 43 years, the restaurant Lutece closed. The owner of the four star restaurant and the first NYC celebrity chef, Andre Soltner, was courtly and suave. He was unpretentious and displayed the classic elegance of the Old World. He offered more than a wonderful meal. He also offered a wonderful dining experience. Think Andre. Give your customers an unforgettable experience that makes them brag, brings them back and encourages referrals. (The same is true for personal relationships.) (paraphrased from The New York Times)

Life expectancy for males retiring today at age 65 is 80.2 years.
Life expectancy for females retiring today at age 65 is 84 years.

Mature individuals have unique needs when compared to younger generations. They make more deliberate decisions. They are not our grandparents. Their self-image is one of mature youth and retained vigor. Most of all, they will go kicking and screaming into old age. As important, the 50 plus group controls most of the nation's wealth.

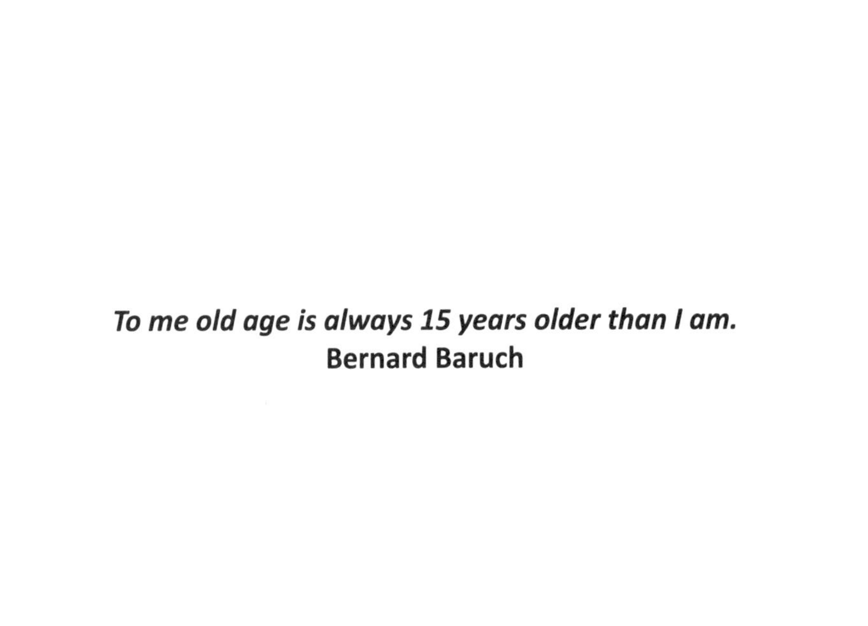

To me old age is always 15 years older than I am.
Bernard Baruch

Like most segments of the population, mature individuals will do business with professionals they perceive as honest, sincere, knowledgeable and trustworthy. They are seeking advice to solve a problem or meet a need. Unlike less experienced individuals, mature individuals "know the ropes," have been "hustled" by the best, and recognize a "con" when they see it. Remain sincere and straightforward. These qualities will make the deal and close the sale. Most of all, it is the right thing to do.

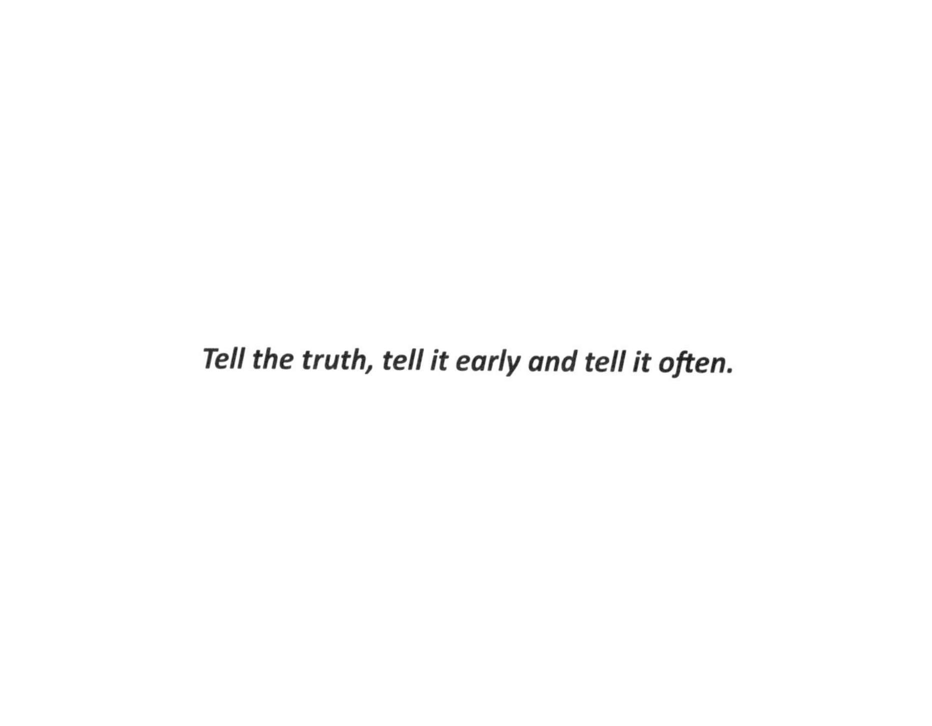

Tell the truth, tell it early and tell it often.

A cover-up can be more damaging than the initial incident. There are numerous examples of embarrassing events that have been compounded by an attempted cover-up. Most problems can be overcome by implementing a direct, cohesive and truthful strategy. Initially, use a noncommittal statement like, "Let me check this out get back to you." The biggest mistake one can make is to misrepresent the situation and combine it with the arrogance that you can "sell the story" despite the contradictory details. The best solution? Tell the truth. Provide a solution. Resolve the issue in a professional manner.

When boasting ends, dignity begins.

Owen D. Young

As you grow older, it is possible to make a fool of yourself in a more dignified manner. If one is lucky, chronological advancement brings maturity, patience, understanding and the ability to overlook others' transgressions. Try to ignore circumstances that are not important. Otherwise you will not only be a curmudgeon, but an aging curmudgeon.

Many individuals take pride in being stupid.
Unfortunately many have already been elected.

It is impossible to win an argument with an ignorant man. Some individuals just don't want to be confused with the facts or consider another view. In English pubs the tradition is for individuals to sit around the table to debate opposing views in a civil and mannerly tone. The conversation is a friendly discourse with no hard feelings for the opponent. Unfortunately in many debates, when one disagrees, one does not have a differing opinion but a wrong opinion. Not always, but too often true.

Patience, persistence and perspiration make an unbeatable combination for success.

Napoleon Hill

If you want to know where you are going, you need to know where you are now. Sometimes quick actions are required, but hopefully the decisions are not earthshaking in your life. It matters little whether you order steak or chicken for dinner. It does matter when you make a decision that has a material effect on your personal life or your career. The ideal approach is to methodically approach major decisions by gathering the facts, evaluating the information, removing the emotion, and making the decision.

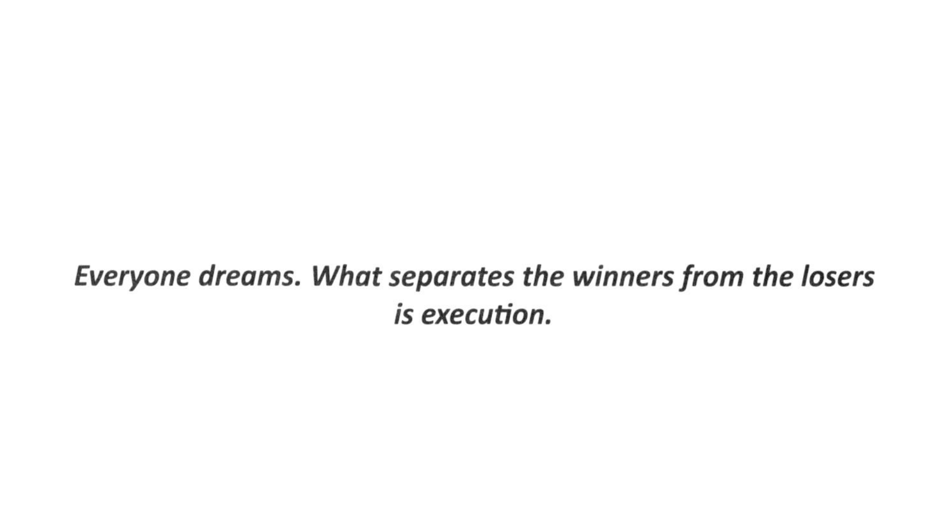

Everyone dreams. What separates the winners from the losers is execution.

Finding a solution may be complicated but the approach to success should be simple and structured. Determine what you want to accomplish, propose various solutions, select the most viable, determine your target market, formalize the approach and proceed with the project. The solution is effort and action.

Accept the challenge so that you can feel the exhilaration of victory.
General George S. Patton

There are specific steps to analyzing a challenge. They include quality, cost, efficient production, consistent performance and a product or service that meets the needs of the consumer at a price they can afford and a price they are willing to pay.

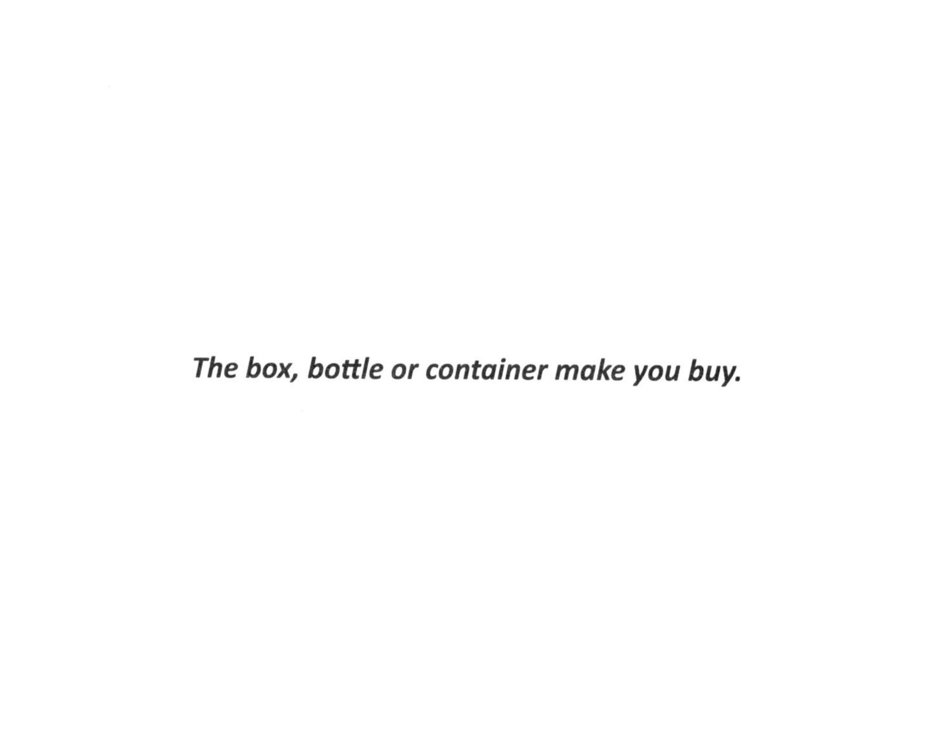

The box, bottle or container make you buy.

What is your high margin franchise? Most companies have a few wheel horse products. Here is food for thought. Less inventory means more profitability. A parts supply company offering 1,000 parts determined that 95% of their business was from selling 100 different parts. They reduced the inventory by 90 percent. This action lowered expenses, improved shipping time, enhanced morale and increased profits exponentially. Point being: look to improve productivity, efficiency, profit and morale.

Trust men and they will be true to you;
treat them greatly and they will show themselves great.
Ralph Waldo Emerson

A Few Thoughts From **Lou Holtz**

Motivation is simple. You eliminate those who are not motivated.
When all is said and done, more is said than done.
Don't be a spectator, don't let life pass you by.
You never get ahead of anyone as long as you try to get even with him.
The man who complains about the way the ball bounces is likely the one who dropped it.

The very best impromptu speeches are the ones written well in advance.

Ruth Gordon

A recent survey indicates that most individuals are apprehensive about making a formal presentation. The key to a successful presentation is preparation and practice. Most anxiety is eliminated when you know your information "cold." Many presenters, including professionals, are nervous the first few minutes but quickly gain confidence and are dynamic. That can be you. A few hints on how to make your speech easier. Visit the room before you speak. Stand behind the podium to get a "feel" for the room. Have formal notes well spaced and in large type. Arrive early and meet the audience. Look your audience in the eye. Most of all, know your material. It is not that difficult if you are prepared.

One goal of a winner is to demonstrate perfect manners and great charm.

BW

A true champion acts like a champion. While you may still hoist the championship trophy, you also need to behave in a courteous manner. People like a gracious winner. When acknowledging your triumph, remain humble. Praise the competition and thank everyone. Also, be a gracious loser. Compliment the winners and wish them well. You don't have to mean it, just say it. Show proper form. One outburst can eliminate years of good will. Many champions are remembered for their bad manners, not their accomplishments.

Modesty should be typical of the success of a champion.
Major Taylor

If you can do it it's not bragging, but why brag? Without question a highly admired quality is modesty. Often those least deserving of praise are the individuals most often seeking recognition by talking about their accomplishments. They never seem to stop talking in order to show everyone their "smarts." It's easy to appear to be modest. Just keep your mouth shut.

Experience is simply the name we give to our mistakes.
Oscar Wilde

You don't have to be right all the time. Your image will actually be enhanced when you admit that you were incorrect on certain matters, especially issues that have little impact on circumstances but are important to someone. If you are right half the time you will still be considered a genius.

If you can't laugh at yourself, make fun of other people.

Bobby Slayton

Self-deprecation is an approach that will endear you to others more than most anything else. When folks realize you don't take yourself too seriously and you can joke about your short-comings, (not that you have any, of course) you will make friends. Most individuals take themselves too seriously because of their insecurities and pomposity. Neither trait is positive. Relax, have fun, smile a lot, make new friends. If you are charming enough, they might buy lunch.

VOLUME PURCHASES AND DISCOUNTS ARE AVAILABLE

Additional copies of this book can be obtained at the following locations
WinningPublishing@gmail.com
wellsb8787@aol.com
Telephone: 850-449-0879
WPP Books
Gulf Breeze, Florida

PRICE LIST*

1 – 9 copies	$7.95
10 – 25 copies	$7.00
26 – 50 copies	$6.50
51 – 100 copies	$6.00
101 – 499 copies	$5.50
500+ copies	$5.00

*plus S&H and taxes if applicable